SREEMAD BHAGAWAD GEETA

CHAPTER VII

ORIGINAL SANSKRIT TEXT WITH ROMAN TRANSLITERATION,
WORD-FOR-WORD MEANING, TRANSLATION AND COMMENTARY

SWAMI CHINMAYANANDA

CENTRAL CHINMAYA MISSION TRUST
MUMBAI - 400 072

© Central Chinmaya Mission Trust

Printed upto	1990 to March	2007	14,000	copies
Reprint	April	2008	2,000	copies
Reprint	March	2010	3,000	copies

Published by :
CENTRAL CHINMAYA MISSION TRUST
Sandeepany Sadhanalaya,
Saki Vihar Road,
Mumbai   400 072, India
Tel. : (91-22) 2857 2367 / 2857 5806
Fax : (91-22) 2857 3065
E-mail : ccmtpublications@chinmayamission.com
Website : www.chinmayamission.com

Distribution Centre in USA :
CHINMAYA MISSION WEST
Publications Division,
560 Bridgetown Pike,
Langhorne, PA 19053, USA.
Phone : (215) 396-0390
Fax : (215) 396-9710
Email : publications@chinmaya.org
Website : www.chinmayapublications.org

Printed by :
PRASHANT ART PRINTERS
203, Amrut CHS., Ltd., M.G. Road,
Dahanukar Wadi, Kandivli (W),
Mumbai - 400 067.
Tel . : 91-22-6695 9935

Price : Rs : 40=00

ISBN: 978-81-7597-089-2

GEETA CHAPTER VII

KNOWLEDGE AND WISDOM

INTRODUCTION

The eighteen Chapters of the Geeta in the arrangement of their ideas fall into three sets of six chapters each. This is the conclusion arrived at by many Geeta-students. According to them, Geeta, being a book which re-interprets the very essence of the Vedic Law, in the entire scheme of its discussions the Divine Song expresses the Truth of the Mahavakya *"That Thou Art."*

Mahavakyas are four* in number — one taken from each of the four Vedas and they form four definite pointers, all indicating the one and the same sacred Truth, which the Vedas unanimously declare. Of these *"That Thou Art"* *(Tat Twam Asi)* is called the "instruction message" *(Upadesa Vakya)*. This crisp sentence summarises the entire Vedic Law and its philosophy and therefore, voluminous commentaries are necessary to elucidate the true significance of each of these three short words.

According to some reviewers of the Geeta, the first section of the Divine Song comprising the opening six chapters, explains the significance of the term *"Thou" (Twam)*, in the *Mahavakya*. The second section, opening with the Seventh Chapter and concluding with the Twelfth, explains the term 'That' *(Tat)* in the same declaration. From this chapter on-

---

* The four Mahavakyas are: "Consciousness is Brahman" *(Pragyanam Brahma)*, "That thou art" *(Tat-Twam-Asi)*; "This Atman is Brahman" *(Ayam Atma Brahma)*, "I am Brahman" *(Aham Brahma-Smi)*.

wards, therefore, we will be gaining a true glimpse of the goal of the spiritual science, as indicated in the Hindu cultural tradition. The last six chapters naturally express the meaning of the term "Art" *(Asi)* and explain the identity of That-essence and Thou-significance.

This division of the great textbook does not necessarily mean that there is a divorce between the earlier section consti-tuted by the first six chapters and the subsequent sections. There is a criticism against the Geeta that it is a haphazard compilation of the important and attractive stanzas that were available at the time of its compilation, rather hastily done, by perhaps, more than one editor. This is generally voiced by those who have made only a superficial study of this Divine Song. When we give enough thought, and sincerely try to follow the trend of this spiritual discussion between the Master and the student we can easily understand the intimate relationship which exists not only between the stanzas, but also in the logical development of thought from chapter to chapter.

The previous chapter not only gave the technique of Self-realisation through the methods of concentration and meditation but also concluded with Krishna's own personal opinion upon who exactly was the noblest among the different seekers pursuing the different paths. According to the Lord of Brindaban, a meditator who tries to concentrate his mind upon the Self is superior to those who strive to deny all sense enjoyment to this body *(Tapaswi)*, or to those who make deep and learned investigations into the scriptural literature *(Gyani)*, or to those who have dedicated themselves to selfless service of the society *(Karmi)*. The Flute-Bearer had again tried to express his opinion, as to who among the meditators, is the most noble. It was declared in the concluding stanza of the previous chapter that of all the meditators, the one who has successfully merged his mind in the nature of the Pure Consciousness, through the path of single-pointed meditation, is the highest and the dearest.

Naturally, there would be a possible doubt, in the mind of Arjuna as to how a limited and mortal mind-and-intellect of a finite creature could ever embrace and comprehend the entire limitless Infinite. In order to remove his doubt, Krishna opens this particular chapter, now under our pen, with a promise that he will explain to Arjuna the entire science, both in its theoretical and speculative aspects, and clear all his possible doubts on the subject. Indeed, for exhaustiveness in treatment and thoroughness in exposition there is, perhaps, no other religious textbook that can stand a favourable comparison with the Geeta. In this sense of the term, we should appreciate the Geeta, not only as a textbook of our philosophy, but also as a literary masterpiece of beauty and erudition in the world's literature.

मय्यासक्तमनाः पार्थ योगं युञ्जन्मदाश्रयः ।
असंशयं समग्रं मां यथा ज्ञास्यसि तच्छृणु ॥ १ ॥

Sri Bhagavan Uvacha

1.   *mayy asaktamanah partha   yogam yunjan madasrayah*
     asamsayam samagram mam   yatha jnasyasi tac chrnu

मयि — On Me, आसक्तमनाः— with mind intent, पार्थ —
O Partha, योगम् — Yoga, युञ्जन् — practising, मदाश्रयः —
taking refuge in Me, असंशयं— without doubt, समग्रम्—wholly,
माम् — Me, यथा — how, ज्ञास्यसि — shalt know, तत् — that,
शृणु — hear.

   1. *With the mind intent on Me, O Partha, practising Yoga*
and taking refuge in Me, how thou shalt, without doubt, know
Me fully, that do thou hear.

It would be, naturally, the doubt of all seekers, especially
before they enter the seat of meditation as to how it was
possible for a limited mind to understand or embrace the
unlimited. This doubt can come to such seekers, who try only
for intellectual appreciation of the philosophy of Vedanta;
but all seekers could only be, in the beginning, mere scholarly
students of the Vedantic literature. This is an unavoidable
stage in the Path of Knowledge. The Science of Vedanta
exhaustively deals with this problem and tries to explain how
the mind, when made to meditate upon the Infinite, comes to
transcend its own limitations and experience the Infinite.

Here Krishna introducing the theme to be dealt with the
next six chapters, guarantees Arjuna that He will explain the
entire science and technique which will clearly show how a

meditator by fixing his integrated mind upon the contemplation of the nature of the Self, can come to experience the Divine. From this chapter onwards the term 'mind' is to be understood, not as a debilitated and disintegrated mind, but as an integrated mind properly tutored to walk, implicitly obeying the will of the discriminative intellect. When such a mind is firmly established in full concentration upon the divine nature of its Godly potentialities, the seeker evolves double quick. The logic of this inward development, it is promised, would be theme of this section.

Now listen to what I am going to say as to how you also, thus acting, will, without doubt, know Me in full, possessed of Infinite greatness, strength, grace and other attributes.

ज्ञानं तेऽहं सविज्ञानमिदं वक्ष्याम्यशेषतः ।
यज्ज्ञात्वा नेह भूयोऽन्यज्ज्ञातव्यमवशिष्यते ॥ २ ॥

2. *jnanam te 'ham savijnanam   idam vaksyamy asesatah
yaj jnatva ne 'ha bhuyo'nyaj   jnatavyam avasisyate*

ज्ञानम् –Indirect knowledge of Sastras, ते — to thee, अहम्—I, सविज्ञानम् — combined with realisation (direct knowledge of Atma through experience), इदम् — this, वक्ष्यामि— will declare, अशेषतः— in full, यत् — which, ज्ञात्वा— having known, न — not, इह — here, भूयः— more, अन्यत् — anything else, ज्ञातव्यम् — what ought to be known, अवशिष्यते — remains.

2. *I shall declare to thee in full this knowledge combined with realisation, which being known, nothing more here remains to be known.*

As an introduction of this section, constituted of the following six Chapters, Krishna promises that he will be delivering hereunder the entire Hindu Philosophy, both the speculative and the practical, in such an exhaustive fashion that nothing more shall remain to be added which was worth knowing. It is always the practice in preserving all patent secrets that the owner of the secret only gives out either the theoretical explanation or, if at all he gives the details of the unto himself, so that he may still have the monopoly of the right knowledge in all its entirety.

A modern example of the above can be found in the explanation of the atom secrets. The atom-scientists give us some theoretical explanation of the nuclear science, the constitution of the energy-particles in an atom, and even openly give out the mathematical calculations of the enormous amount of energy contained in each atom. But, except for the rudimentary principles of the construction of the Atom Bomb, they do not give the complete secret to all. Similarly, he it will be doubted that the technique and science of perfection may not be exhaustively and completely given out by the Lord in the Geeta, as vividly as it is in the Upanishads. This doubt is quite justified because the Geeta comes in the midst of the great classic of the world, the Maha-Bharata. Here, Krishna endorses and guarantees that the Geeta is a total and exhaustive summary of the philosophy of the Upanishads and though it reads as simple and elementary, in its import and deeper significance, the Divine Song exhausts the entire Knowledge.

According to Sankara, speculative knowledge, is *Gyana* and actual experience of the perfection is *Vigyana*. Here Krishna is promising that he shall not only deliver to Arjuna the theoretical explanations of the Art of Divine Life but also during the very discourse, take him to the highest peak of Self-rediscovery. This may look rather unbelievable but unlike *Yoga* and other methods of philosophies in India, Vedanta is not an indirect process, inasmuch as, after the study of the *Sastra,* it is not necessary for a fit student to retire into the jungles to practise and bring the experience of perfection into his cognition.

During the very discourse, if the student is mentally fit to walk along with the teacher step by step and follow carefully the logic and significance of his explanations, he can gain glimpses of realisation during the very hours of his study. It is because of this that Vedanta is taught only to a student who has been made fit for this flight to the beyond. If inwardly an individual student is perfectly integrated and if the student can maintain continuously his adventurous thirst to experience the Reality, that student, in his attempt to identify himself with the thought and the spirit of his teacher's discourses, can ultimately come to revel in the experience of the very goal that is indicated by Vedanta. Self realisation is instantaneous during the understanding of scripture gained through the teacher-taught discussion.

If Vedanta is thus a complete Science and the experience of the Divinity of the Self can be had even during the very teacher-taught discussions how is it that self-realised masters are so rare in the world ! Listen :—

मनुष्याणां सहस्रेषु कश्चिद्यतति सिद्धये ।
यततामपि सिद्धानां कश्चिन्मां वेत्ति तत्त्वतः ॥ ३ ॥

3. *manusyanam sahasresu   kascid yatati siddhaye*
    yatatam api siddhanam   kascin mam vetti tattvatah

मनुष्याणाम् — Of men, सहस्रेषु — among thousands, कश्चित् – some one, यतति — strives, सिद्धये — for perfection, यतताम्—

of the striving ones, अपि— even. सिद्धानां— of the successful ones, कश्चित्– some one, माम् — Me. वेति— knows, तत्त्वतः—in essence.

3. *Among thousands of men, one perchance strives for perfection; even among those successful strivers, only one perchance knows Me in essence.*

Hearing this seemingly outrageous statement from Krishna, that Vedanta or self-realisation is as easy as listening to a short story telling, Arjuna got confused, because, this assertion of the Lord conflicted with his tutored ideas regarding the Hindu theory of Self-perfection. Naturally, his eyes, as it were, bulge out expressing his bewilderment. Krishna has, therefore, to explain why in spite of the fact that Self-realisation was so simple and easy, it did not come within the experience of everyone. This stanza explains why the majority still choose to remain in the area of ignorance to weep and to sigh, and are not able to walk into the lit-up arena of Perfect Knowledge and inward equanimity.

The idea that Vedantic realisation and knowledge can come to the experience of only a rare few, has been repeatedly emphasized in different portions of the spiritual literature in India, by different Masters, in different expressions. We were told previously how the very theoretical side of Vedanta is heard and understood as a marvel.* In the Upanishads also, the same idea has been very clearly expressed by the Rishis.**

Here, however, Krishna shifts the entire responsibility for not realising the Self upon the individual seeker himself

---

* Please refer Chapter II-29.
** Please refer Swamiji's *Discourses on Kathopanishad*-I — (ii) — 7.

and attributes it entirely to the Sadhak's lack of self-application. Vedanta being a subjective science, it is not only sufficient that we must know how to eradicate our weaknesses and cultivate our inward strength, but we must also live up to those ideals and try to bring about the necessary re-adjustments in ourselves. Very few can discover in themselves, this necessary urge to evolve.

Of the thousands that hear intelligently, and perhaps understand all the theory and text of the Vedanta, only a few sincerely apply themselves to live fully the Vedantic way-of-life. Even among a thousand such sincere seekers, only a rare few *"come to know Me in My real nature"*.

The chances are that when this Vedantic way of life is perfectly explained by a *Sad-Guru* to student, who is seemingly attending with all enthusiasm, sincerity and concentration, he may raise himself up to, perhaps, the very Gates of Truth, but there, he himself may come to bar his own entry into the 'within'. Some imperceptible vanity or unsuspected desire is sufficient there, to exile him from himself. In this sense, there is a wealth of meaning in Lord Christ's declaration that a camel can pass through the eye of a needle more easily than a rich man through the gates of heaven — the riches are not the 'worldly wealth', but the individual mental *Vasana*-wealth. Unless the mind is perfectly naked, it has no entry into the Bliss of Truth.

By thus showing the extreme difficulty of attaining Self-realisation, it is not intended that the students of Vedanta should feel disappointed and desperate. The stanza should not be read as a pessimistic declaration. Krishna in the entire Mahabharata is painted as a living embodiment of cheer and laughter, a man of inexhaustible hope and joy. Of all the

Godly personalities in the history of the religious literature of the world, if at all there be one character that has not as much as felt a mental depression, it is the Flute-Bearer of Brindaban. Such a master, especially when he is trying to encourage his friend who is in despondency, cannot be considered as offering Arjuna a dose of extra pessimism.

Viewing the stanza in the light of the Krishna-spirit, it only means that rare indeed are people who come to study sincerely and get a true glimpse of the Vedanta-literature, and only a very low percentage of these again can discover in themselves the necessary mental stamina, the intellectual vision and the physical forbearance to live that life of truth and purity in the world. Since Arjuna and all the students of the Geeta are such rare souls, they represent the community of evolvers. To them Krishna promises that He can, through His Divine Song not only deliver the speculative part of the philosophy of Vedanta but also practically hand over chances to live subjectively vital moments of vivid inward experience of the Self.

Having prepared the hearer for the teaching by inducing in him a taste for it, the Lord proceeds thus :—

भूमिरापोऽनलो वायुः खं मनो बुद्धिरेव च ।
अहंकार इतीयं मे भिन्ना प्रकृतिरष्टधा ॥ ४ ॥

4. *bhumir apo 'nalo vayuh   kham mano buddhir eva ca
    ahamkara iti'yam me   bhinna prakrtir astadha*

भूमिः — Earth, आपः — water, अनलः — fire, वायुः — air, खम् — ether, मनः — mind, बुद्धिः — intellect, एव — even, च — and, अहङ्कारः — egoism, इति — thus, इयम् — this, मे — My, प्रकृतिः — nature, भिन्ना — divided, अष्टधा — eightfold.

4. *Earth, water, fire, air, ether, mind, intellect, egoism —*
thus is My eightfold Prakriti.

In an attempt to explain the world outside as a marriage between matter and Spirit, great thinkers of the Vedic period had exhausted their philosophical acumen and had given us the Sankhya Philosophy. According to them, the Spiritual Factor *(Purusha)* presiding over a given matter envelopment, dynamises the inert matter and makes the insentient mineral assembly to act, as though it is intelligent and vital. This idea becomes clear to us when we take an example from the modern world.

With steel and iron the manufacturer completes a steam-engine and when the cold engine is harnessed to steam, at high pressure, it does work. Steam by itself can never express its dynamic capacity and strength; on the other hand, when it is made to work through a given equipment, it is capable of adding movement and motion to the inert iron assemblage.

Similarly, one school of philosophy in India tries to explain, scientifically, how the Eternal and the Perfect comes to express Itself as a world of plurality, in the embrace of matter. This also explains the relationship between the Spirit and matter. The technical terms used in the philosophy for these two items are *Prakriti,* for the matter envelopments, and *Purusha* for the Spirit-factor.

Krishna explains in this and the following stanza, what all items together constitute the matter-part in us and what exactly constitutes the Spiritual Entity within a living man. Once the individual comes to understand, clearly and distinctly, the distinction between matter and Spirit, indeed, he will come to understand that the Spirit identifying with matter, is the cause for all Its sufferings and when It is detached from all Its identifications, It rediscovers for Itself Its own essential nature as Perfection and Bliss Absolute. The Spirit identifying with matter and sharing the destinies of the inert equipment is called the Ego. It is the Ego that rediscovers itself to be nothing other than the Spirit that presides over the matter.

In order to make Arjuna realise how exactly one is to understand the true nature of the Self, in all its divine might and glory, Lord Krishna tries to enumerate the matter-aspect, as distinct from the Spiritual-Truth in each individual.

The five Great Elements, Mind, Intellect and Ego constitute, according to the Geeta, the eight-fold *Prakriti* that has come to be super-imposed upon the Truth through Ignorance. The five Great Cosmic Elements are represented in the Microcosm by the five sense organs by which the individual comes to experience and live in the world of sense-objects. Thus, the list making up the *Prakriti* is nothing other than the subtle body and its vehicles of expression constituted of the sense-organs. The sense-organs are the channels through which the world of stimuli reaches within and the inner point of focus of the five sense-organs is called the Mind. The impulses received in the mind are rationally classified and systematised into the knowledge of their reception by the intellect. At all these three levels of the sense perception, mental reception, and intellectual assimilation there is a continuous sense of I-ness, which is called the Ego. These constitute the equipment through which, at the touch of Life, man functions as the intelligent being that he is.

What then is your higher nature? Listen :—

अपरेयमितस्त्वन्यां प्रकृतिं विद्धि मे पराम् ।
जीवभूतां महाबाहो ययेदं धार्यते जगत् ॥ ५ ॥

5. *apare 'yam itas tv anyam   prakrtim viddhi me param*
jivabhutam mahabaho   yaye dam dharyate jagat

अपरा — Lower, इयम् — this, इतः— from this, तु — but,
अन्याम् — different, प्रकृतिम्— nature, विद्धि— know, मे — My,
पराम् — higher, जीवभूताम् — the very life-element, महाबाहो —
O mightily-armed, यया — by which, इदम् — this, धार्यते —
is upheld, जगत् — world.

5. *This is the inferior (Prakriti) but different from it,
know thou, O mighty-armed, My higher Prakriti, the very
life-element, by which this world is upheld.*

After enumerating in the above stanza the Lower Nature
of the Self, Krishna says that it is not all and that the Self-
possesses, besides these equipments, a Higher Nature which
is constituted of Pure Consciousness or Awareness. It is the
Spiritual Entity that makes it possible for the body, mind and
intellect, made up of the mere inert minerals, to act as if they
were in themselves so vitally sentient and intelligent.

The Spiritual Factor is the Entity with whose contact the
equipment functions, but without which, the equipment becomes dull and insentient. If Consciousness were not in us, we
will not be able to experience the world outside or within us. It
is this Consciousness that maintains, nourishes, and sustains
all the possibilities in us. Without this Spiritual Spark functioning in us, we would be no more intelligent or divine than
the stone world.

Even by a more material consideration, we can logically
come to accept the conclusions declared in this stanza. I am

standing on the floor of my house; the house is supported by
my piece of land; the land is protected by the Delhi Corpora-
tion; Delhi is supported by India; India is supported by the
World; the world is supported by water — the waters of the
ocean; water is held in position by the atmosphere and the
atmosphere is a part of the planetary system. The Universe
stays in space, and this space rests upon the "concept of
space" that is in our mind. Mind gets its support from the
judgement of the intellect. Since the decision of the intellect is
known and realised by the Consciousness in us, the Spiritual
Entity is the ultimate support for the entire *Jagat*.

In philosophy, the term *Jagat* means not only the world of
objects perceived by us through our sense-organs but it inc-
ludes in its concept, the world experienced through and inter-
preted by the mind and intellect also. Thus the world-of-
objects, the world-of-feelings and the world-of-ideas that we
experience together, in their totality, constitute the *Jagat*.
This is supported by the Conscious Principle with Its grace
showering upon them all. In this sense also, Krishna's declarations are scientifically true, when He says that the higher
Prakriti, the Principle of Consciousness is that *"by which this
entire world of experiences is sustained"*.

How is the Self the Creator, Sustainer and the Dissolver of
the world? Listen :—

एतद्योनीनि भूतानि सर्वाणीत्युपधारय ।
अहं कृत्स्नस्य जगतः प्रभवः प्रलयस्तथा ॥ ६ ॥

6.   *etadyonini bhutani   sarvani 'ty upadharaya
       aham krtsnasya jagatah   prabhavah pralayas tatha*

एतद्योनीनि — Those (two Prakriti) are the womb of, भूतानि-
beings, सर्वाणि— all, इति— thus, उपधारय— know, अहम्— I,
कृत्स्नस्य — of the whole, जगतः— of the world, प्रभवः— source,
प्रलयः — dissolution, तथा — also.

6. *Know that these (two Prakritis) are the womb of all
beings. So I am the source and dissolution of the whole
universe.*

The above mentioned Higher and Lower Nature, each
functioning in the embrace of the other, cause the manifestation of the world of plurality. If Matter were not there, the
latent dynamism in the Spirit will not find a field for Its
expression. The Matter by itself, in its inertness, will not be
able to express the similitude of Consciousness unless the
Spirit were there to dynamise it. Electricity expressing itself
through the filament in the bulb manifests as light. Without
the bulb the light in the electricity cannot manifest itself nor
can the bulb smile forth in light without the electrical current
flowing through it. The bulb is the equipment, functioning
through which, electricity expresses itself as light. Similarly,
the Spirit when It comes to function through the five layers of
Matter* discovers for Itself, a field to express Its own
potentialities.

Keeping this idea in mind, Lord Krishna declares here
that *"these two are the womb of all beings."* It is not very
difficult for an intelligent student to realise what it actually
means. Not only that the pluralistic world of objects, feelings,
and ideas rises from, and stays in the spirit but it will dissolve
into It, again to become the Higher-Nature. Thus, the Lower-
Nature is nothing other than the Higher in its essential con-

---

* Please refer 'Swamiji's Meditation and Life'.

stitution. The Higher, forgetting Its own divinity, identifies
Itself with the Lower and comes to the Ego-centric sorrows
and imperfections. The Higher suffers at present, in Its own
delusions, the sorrows of the Lower. Its own rediscovery of Its
native divine glory is the redemption of Matter. The idea that
the Lower has risen from the Higher is likened to the way in
which pots of different shapes and colours have all come from
the mud. Just as the mud is the truth in all the pots, the Higher
is the essential Reality in all the objects of the sense-organs,
mind and intellect which the Lower procreates.

Therefore —

मत्तः परतरं नान्यत्किंचिदस्ति धनंजय ।
मयि सर्वमिदं प्रोतं सूत्रे मणिगणा इव ॥ ७ ॥

7.   *mattah parataram na 'nyat   kimcid asti dhananjaya*
     mayi sarvam idam protam   sutre manigana iva

मत्तः— Than Me, परतरम्— higher, न— not, अन्यत्—
other, किंचित्— anyone, अस्ति— is, धनंजय— O Dhananjaya,
मयि— in Me, सर्वम्— all, इदम्— this, प्रोतम्— is strung,
सूत्रे— on a string, मणिगणाः— clusters of gems, इव— like.

7. *There is nothing whatsoever higher than Me,
O Dhananjaya. All this is strung in Me, as clusters of gems on a
string.*

There are two possible points of view of our life if the
above mentioned theory is accepted. There is a point of view
from the Lower and distinctly different from it, there is
another point of view of life from the Higher also. Just as in
the mud there is none of the different shapes and colours of
the pots, so too in the Pure Consciousness there is none of the
worlds of objects, feelings and ideas. *"Besides Me there is*

naught.'' After waking up to the waker, there is nothing of the dream-world for his recognition. In the endless waves that rise in the ocean there is nothing other than the ocean itself. None of the waves can rise, nor stay, nor can ultimately reach anywhere but the ocean itself. In short, nothing can remain ever totally divorced from its own essential Nature.

The first indicates that each one of us has a Lower-Nature which is married to our own Self but still, the doubt might come into the minds of the students of the Geeta, that the Self in me is different from the Self in all others. This logic of thinking may, as a result, come to the conclusion that there are as many different Selves as there are different bodies in the world. To show that the Self is one and the same in all the forms, it has been said here that the Lord is the common factor, in all forms in the universe. He holds them all intact as a chord holds the pearls in a necklace. These words have deep significance. Not only that it is beautiful in its poetic suggestion but it has also a very exhaustive philosophical indication. The pearls in the necklace are necessarily uniform and homogeneous and its thread, which is generally unseen, passes through the geometrical core of every pearl and holds the big and the small into a harmonious thing of beauty. Again, the substance of which the pearls are made is totally different from the constituents that go to make the thread. Similarly, the worlds are all held together by the Spiritual Truth into a complete whole. Even in an individual, the mind, the intellect, the body, each different from one another can harmoniously work and unitedly give the music of life for him because the same Conscious Principle works through all these different and varying matter envelopments.

Here is an instance where we see Shri Veda Vyasa typically represented as the poet philosopher of the world. This example is not only poetical but also deeply philosophical.

Further —

रसोऽहमप्सु कौन्तेय प्रभास्मि शशिसूर्ययोः ।
प्रणवः सर्ववेदेषु शब्दः खे पौरुषं नृषु ॥ ८ ॥

8. *raso 'ham apsu kaunteya prabha 'smi sasisuryayoh*
     pranavah sarvavedesu sabdah khe paurusam nrsu

रसः — Sapidity, अहम् — I, अप्सु — in water, कौन्तेय —
O Kaunteya (son of Kunti), प्रभा — light, अस्मि — am (I),
शशिसूर्ययोः — in the moon and the Sun, प्रणवः — the syllable
OM, सर्ववेदेषु — in all the Vedas, शब्दः — sound, खे — in ether,
पौरुषम् — virility, नृषु — in men.

8. *I am the sapidity in water, O son of Kunti, I am the light
in the moon and the sun; I am the syllable OM in all the Vedas,
sound in ether, and virility in men.*

पुण्यो गन्धः पृथिव्यां च तेजश्चास्मि विभावसौ ।
जीवनं सर्वभूतेषु तपश्चास्मि तपस्विषु ॥ ९ ॥

9. *punyo gandhah prthivyam ca tejas ca 'smi vibhavasau*
     jivanam sarvabhutesu tapas ca 'smi tapasvisu

पुण्यः — Sweet, गन्धः — fragrance, पृथिव्याम् — in earth,
च — and, तेजः — brilliance, च — and, अस्मि — am (I),
विभावसौ — in fire, जीवनम् — life, सर्वभूतेषु — in all beings,
तपः — austerity, च — and, अस्मि — and (I), तपस्विषु — in the
austere.

9. *I am the sweet fragrance in earth and the brilliance in
the fire, the life in all beings, and I am austerity in the austere.*

How the Supreme Self could be the thread upon which the pearls consisting of individual plurality are strung together to become the necklace of the harmonious universe, is described in these two stanzas. It has been already said, *"My Higher Prakriti, the Principle of Consciousness"*, is the womb of all beings and that *"beyond Me there is naught"*. What this Eternal Factor which is common in every one and yet not readily perceptible to all could be is the doubt that has been cleared here.

That which remains in a substance from the beginning to the end, constantly, and without which the thing cannot ever maintain its identity, is called its *Dharma* — which is its "law of being". The examples of 'sapidity in watery', 'radiance in the sun and the moon', 'Om in all Vedas', 'sound in *Akasa*', 'sweet smell in Earth', 'luminosity in Fire', 'manhood in man', and 'austerity in the austere' — all clearly indicate that the Self is that which gives each individual phenomenon its own existence. In short, as the stanza declares, the Self is the *Life in all beings*.

As more vivid example for grosser intellects the Lord gives the following set of examples :—

बीजं मां सर्वभूतानां विद्धि पार्थ सनातनम् ।
बुद्धिर्बुद्धिमतामस्मि तेजस्तेजस्विनामहम् ॥ १ ० ॥

10. *bijam mam sarvabhutanam   viddhi partha sanatanam*
    buddhir buddhimatam asmi   tejastejasvinam aham

बीजम् — Seed, माम् — Me, सर्वभूतानाम् — of all beings, विद्धि: — know, पार्थ — O Partha, सनातनम्— eternal, बुद्धि:— intelligence, बुद्धिमताम् — of the intelligent, अस्मि — am (I), तेज:— splendour, तेजस्विनाम् — of the splendid, अहम् — I.

10. *Know Me, O Partha, as the eternal seed of all beings; I am the intelligence of the intelligent; the splendour of the splendid (things and beings), am I.*

Not satisfied with above enumeration, which can truly indicate its full significances only to those who have a fairly good amount of subtle intelligence, the Lord is compelled to indicate the same Truth through some other more obvious examples. He says in the stanza, *"I am the ancient seed of all beings"*. Not satisfied, again, with this statement, as an artist would mix more colours afresh and paint, again and again, to bring out his theme more vividly to the perception of the on-lookers, Bhagavan here gives two more beautiful instances by which we can get an insight into the relationship between the gross perceivable Matter and the imperceptible Spirit.

"I am the intellect of the intelligent" : The intelligent man constantly expresses a greater amount of divinity in his thoughts and ideas. In that intelligent man, the Self is the intelligence, that subtle Power because of which the individual is capable of manifesting such brilliant intelligence. Similarly, it is also said that the Self is that which beams out through the beautiful and the energetic.

In other words, through the instrument of our intellect, it is the Consciousness in us that expresses itself as an intelligent individual. As a parallel we can say that electricity is "the light in the bulb"; is 'the heat in the heater'; is 'the music in the radio'.

Yet another example is given in the following :—

बलं बलवतामस्मि कामरागविवर्जितम् ।
धर्माविरुद्धो भूतेषु कामोऽस्मि भरतर्षभ ॥ ११ ॥

11. *balam balavatam asmi   kamaragavivarjitam*
     dharmaviruddho bhutesu   kamo 'smi bharatarsabha

बलम् — Strength, बलवताम् — Of the strong, अस्मि — am
(I), कामरागविवर्जितम् — devoid of desire and attachment,
धर्माविरुद्ध — unopposed to Dharma, भूतेषु — in beings, कामः –
desire, भरतर्षभ — O Lord of the Bharatas, अस्मि — am (I).

11. *Of the strong, I am the strength — devoid of desire
and attachment, and in (all) beings, I am the desire — unopposed to Dharma, O best among the Bharatas.*

Having thus served with different examples the seekers
of the *average* intelligence* and the dullest,** here, in this
stanza, the Lord is trying to indicate the Eternal Self to the
most intelligent students, who have the capacity to do subtle
reflection upon such philosophical ideologies.

"I am the strength in the strong": This statement is evidently as easy of comprehension as the example given in the
previous stanza. But the statement out-shines the above set of
examples when, here, Krishna gives the phrase qualifying
"Balam". Generally, an individual expresses his might and
strength only when he is goaded by his desires or attachments.

Without these two inner urgencies, it is impossible for us
to see any expression of might or strength. Desire *(Kama)* and
attachment *(Raga)* are generally considered by students of the
Vedic literature as almost synonyms; but Sankara, in his
commentary, has very thoughtfully given us the distinction
between these two powerful impulses. He says *Kama* is 'desire
for what is absent' at present in the scheme of our life, and

---
* *Ibid* 9.
** *Ibid* 10.

Raga is 'affection for what one has obtained'. These are the two emotions, lashed up by which, individuals or communities, or societies or nations, generally come to express their might and strength *(Balam)*. Riots and agitations, battles and wars, are all ever motivated by these two sources. In the subtle definition of the Self, the Lord here brings a new line of thought for the contemplation of the seeker. He says, the Self is not merely the strength in the strong but *"I am the strength devoid of desire and attachment."*

As though not satisfied with his own definition, the Lord gives yet another example. *"I am desire in the beings unopposed to Dharma"*. We have already explained the term Dharma as the 'Law of being'. The essential Factor in man is the Divine Consciousness. All actions, thoughts and ideas entertained by him which are not opposed to the essence of his divine nature constitute his *Dharma*. All actions and thoughts and ideas entertained by him which are not opposed to the essence of his divine nature constitute his *Dharma*. All actions and thoughts that hasten the evolution of man to rediscover his essential Divine Nature are considered righteous-actions, while all activities of the mind and intellect that take him away from his true Divine Nature and make him behave as though he was an animal and degrade him in his evolutionary status, are called unrighteous behaviour.

With this understanding of the term *Dharma*, the second line of the stanza becomes very clear. *"All desires that are not unrighteous for the being"*, means, therefore, the glorious urge in the *evolvers* to meet courageously their own inner weaknesses and bring out a complete consummation of their evolutionary urge, to seek and to discover, the Goal of Self-perfection. This is the subtle power that is indicated here. The Lord says that 'I am not the Sadhak but I am, in him, his burning aspiration to discover and become one with the Immutable Self.'

By the above examples does it mean that the Spirit has been really captured and jailed in by the Matter? How can the limited limit the unlimited! Listen :—

ये चैव सात्त्विका भावा राजसास्तामसाश्च ये ।
मत्त एवेति तान्विद्धि न त्वहं तेषु ते मयि ॥ १ २ ॥

12. *ye cai 'va sattvika bhava   rajasas tamasas ca ye
     matta eve 'ti tan viddhi   na tv aham tesu te mayi*

ये — Whatever, च — and, एव — even, सात्त्विकाः— pure, भावाः — natures, राजसाः — active, तामसाः — inert, च — add, ये — whatever, मत्तः — from Me, एव — even, इति — thus, तान् — them, विद्धि — know, न — not, तु— indeed, अहम् — I, तेषु — in them, ते — they, मयि— in Me.

12. *Whatever beings (and objects) that are pure, active and inert, know them to proceed from Me, yet I am not in them, they are in Me.*

In this stanza, the Lord concludes the topic of His discussion, which He undertook while commenting upon His own statement, *"all this is strung in Me as a row of pearls on a thread"*.

The term *Maya*, as used in the Vedantic literature, is nothing other than the different impulses under which the mind and intellect of the living kingdom come to act. The infinite variety of thoughts and ideas that rise in the hearts of the living kingdom have been observed and classified under the three main moods, governed by which alone do the instruments of feeling, thinking and action come to play their parts everywhere. These three characteristic, eternal moods of the subtle body, are called unactivity *(Sattva)*, activity *(Rajas)*, and inactivity *(Tamas)*.

With this knowledge of the three *Gunas,* as they are called, when we try to understand the stanza, it becomes very easy reading. Whatever states pertaining to these three easy temperaments of the heart and the head are possible, they all rise from the Self, is a statement which is only a re-interpretation, in philosophical terminology of what has been already explained to us. The Infinite Consciousness is the Supreme Reality, the Spirit, upon which the matter, constituting Its lower-Nature, is but an *apparent* experience. They all rise from the Truth, inasmuch as all the waves rise from the ocean; all mud-pots rise from the mud; all ornaments made of god come from gold.

This verse concludes with a beautiful statement which reads like a conundrum. Such an arresting statement is an art deliberately indulged in by the Hindu philosophical writers. This has the charm that invites an independent, intellectual investigation by the student, all by himself, upon the declaration, in order that he may find the sweet secret of its true import and significance. *"Still I am not in them, they are in Me".*

Such a statement would necessarily be false in any situation because, if A is not in B, the latter cannot be in the former — if 'I am not in them, they *cannot* be in me'. This sweet paradoxical statement clearly indicates that the relationship between the Spirit and matter is not in terms of a cause and its effect, but it is only as a super-imposition of matter upon the Spirit. To the deluded the post can only explain, "The ghost of your vision has risen from me, inasmuch as I alone lend to it its existence; but I, the post, am not in the ghost". So, too, shall the ocean carry, "The wave rise, stay and dissolve in me; but I am not in the waves".

As Sankara would have it, the Self declares here that even though matter depends entirely for its existence upon the Conscious Principle, yet the Divine Spark is in no way under the thraldom of matter. Matter ekes out its existence from the Spirit; but, the Spirit is — in no way, at no time, howsoever little — controlled, contaminated or shackled by the sad lot of the finite imperfect matter.

In the following stanza Lord Krishna regrets that the world is not understanding Him in His pure Nature. "What is this ignorance on the part of the world due to?" Listen:—

त्रिभिर्गुणमयैर्भावैर्वैरोभिः सर्वमिदं जगत् ।
मोहितं नाभिजानाति मामेभ्यः परमव्ययम् ॥ १३ ॥

13. *tribhir gunamayair bhavair   ebhih sarvam idam jagat
     mohitaṁ na 'bhijanati   mam ebhyah param avyayam*

त्रिभिः — By three, गुणमयः— composed of Gunas, भावैः — by natures, एभिः— by these, सर्वम् — all, इदम् — this, जगत् — world, मोहितम् — deluded, न — not, अभिजानाति — knows, माम् — Me, एभ्यः— from them, परम् — higher, अव्ययम्— Immutable.

13. *Deluded by these natures (states or things) composed of the three* Gunas *(of* Prakriti) *all this world knows Me not as Immutable and distinct from them.*

If there be such a Divine Factor, beyond the usual cognition of the ordinary mortals, how is it that they are not in a position to understand, atleast the presence, if not completely realise this great Truth? This question is answered here in this verse, *"Deluded by the modifications of the three Gunas"*, the worlds of living creatures become blind to the divine possibilities in themselves and live totally in a life of mere identification with the matter envelopments. The post is covered by the ghost-vision for the deluded. It is a fact that as long as the Ghost is viewed, not even a portion of the post will be available for the perception of the deluded.

Similarly, identifying with the Maya-products, the Self comes to play the tragic role of the Ego, and the Ego, in its own preoccupations with the outer-world and with its own idle imaginations, finds itself incapable of knowing its own true nature. This play of hide-and-seek — ourselves with ourselves in ourselves — is the strange and mysterious play of the ego, in universal sorrow and endless mental squalor.

Thus deluded, the Ego does not realise the Supreme as distinctly different from both the lower and the higher *Prakrities* and experience Its Divine Nature of Immutable glory.

This *"Power of Veiling"* in everyone of us is defined and described in the following stanza.

दैवी ह्येषा गुणमयी मम माया दुरत्यया ।
मामेव ये प्रपद्यन्ते मायामेतां तरन्ति ते ॥ १४ ॥

14. *daivi hy esa gunamayi   mama maya duratyaya*
    mam eva ye prapadyante   mayam etam taranti te

दैवी — Divine, हि — verily, एषा — this, गुणमयी — made of

Gunas, मम — My, माया — illusion, दुरत्यया — difficult to cross over, माम् — in Me, एव — even, ये — who, प्रपद्यन्ते — take refuge, मायाम् — illusion, एताम् — this, तरन्ति — cross over, ते — they.

14. *Verily, this divine illusion of Mine, made up of* Gunas *(caused by the qualities) is difficult to cross over; those who take refuge in Me alone, come to cross over this illusion.*

Lord Krishna himself admits that it is not easy for any egocentric individual to transcend this delusion in himself which is caused by *'My Maya'*. If a doctor were to come and diagnose a disease and declare that there was no cure for that particular disease, nobody will have the faith to follow that doctor's prescription and advice faithfully. Similarly, here, if Krishna's diagnosis of the world's sorrows and problems is to be defined by a term "Maya" and if the Doctor of the Universe declares that this Maya disease is difficult to cure, nobody would faithfully follow such a sad pessimistic philosophy.

Krishna realises these defects and, therefore, immediately removes any such misconceptions from the minds of the students of the Geeta. Sometimes a doctor will have to use strong words in describing the illness to the patient in order to bring home to the sufferer the seriousness of his malady; so, too, Krishna here is only bringing home to us, by a direct thrust the seriousness of the mental tragedy into which the Supreme has seemingly fallen, to become the finite mortal ego. After declaring the seriousness of the disease and the prescription, he hastens to guarantee a complete cure for the malady of man.

"Those who devote themselves to Me alone" shall cross over their subjective delusion, which has created for man the

objective worlds of sorrows and imperfections. How to do this
has been already explained while discussing the technique of
meditation, in the last chapter. With single-pointed mind, to
contemplate on the Self is the direct path; and in order to walk
this narrow-way, the mind is to be made steady and concen-
trated, through the processes that have already been discussed.*

*Then why all those who meditate upon Thee are not
experiencing Thy Glory?*

न मां दुष्कृतिनो मूढाः प्रपद्यन्ते नराधमाः ।
माययापहृतज्ञाना आसुरं भावमाश्रिताः ॥ १ ५ ॥

15.   *na mam duskrtino mudhah   prapadyante naradhamah
       mayaya pahrtajnana   asuram bhavam asritah*

न — Not, माम् — to Me, दुष्कृतिनः — evil-doers, मूढाः —
the deluded, प्रपद्यन्ते — seek, नराधमाः — the lowest of men,
मायया — by Maya, अपहृतज्ञानाः — deprived of knowledge,
आसुरम् — belonging to demons, भावम् — nature, आश्रिताः —
having taken to.

15. *The evil-doers, the deluded, the lowest of men do not
seek Me; they whose discrimination has been destroyed by their
own delusions follow the ways of the demons.*

The last stanza talked of those who can successfully transcend their own subjective delusion and here, naturally,
Krishna is trying to talk about the negative nature in those
who cannot overcome this delusion to realise the Divine in

---

* Refer commentary on Chapter VI — 14.

themselves. Unless the contrast of ideas is given, the student will not be in a position to understand properly, what exactly are the mind's tendencies and appetites that are the true symptoms of the delusions.

"*Low men deluded and indulging themselves in evil actions follow the path of the devil (Asura) and get themselves deprived of their better discrimination*". We all know that the insignia of the higher evolution in man, compared to the animal kingdom, is nothing other than his rational intellect, which can discriminate between the good and the bad, the high and low, the moral and the immoral. This discriminative awareness is the subtle instrument by which individuals are rendered capable of awakening themselves from the dream of their own imperfections to their own Essential Nature of Absolute Divinity.

This faculty can effectively function only in a bosom that is unagitated by the sense-impulses. The more an individual misunderstands himself to be only a mass of flesh and continuously pants for self-gratification through the sense indulgences, the more he is considered as a sinner. Sin, in this sense, is but a devolutionary action which is not appropriate to the dignity and status of the highest evolutionary glory in man. Sin can be perpetrated only by those who have deluded themselves, believing that they are only masses of flesh, with minds hungry for their emotional satisfactions and intellects trying to assert and express their own ideas. Such people are here called by the Geeta as deluded *(Moodha)*. The way of life, in such deluded men *(Asurabhav)*, has been most exhaustively described to us by indicating the opposite good qualities of the perfect one, the *Daivibhav*, later in the Geeta.*

---

* Refer Chapter XVI — 3.

People reach me through four different approaches.
Listen :—

चतुर्विधा भजन्ते मां जनाः सुकृतिनोऽर्जुन ।
आर्तो जिज्ञासुरर्थार्थी ज्ञानी च भरतर्षभ ॥ १६ ॥

16. *caturvidha bhajante mam   janah sukrtino rjuna*
     arto jijnasur artharthi   jnani ca bharatarsabha

चतुर्विधा — Four kinds, भजन्ते — worship, माम् — Me,
जनाः— people, सुकृतिनः:— virtuous, अर्जुन — O Arjuna, आर्तः —
the distressed, जिज्ञासु:— the seeker of knowledge, अर्थार्थी —
the seeker of wealth, ज्ञानी — the wise, च — and, भरतर्षभ —
O Best among the Bharatas.

16. *Four kinds of virtuous men worship Me, O Arjuna,*
the dissatisfied, the seeker of (systematised) knowledge, the
seeker of wealth and the wise, O Best among the Bharatas.

Since the Self is the source of all existence and energy, all
other apparent activities that are seen at the level of matter,
must come from the same motive force. Every part of a
railway engine is made up of cold iron and if the engine can
run forward carrying along with it a train-load of passengers
and goods, there must be something other then iron that is
giving it the capacity to move. Similarly, when the ego-centric
deluded men, considering themselves to be their body or
mind or intellect, act in the world outside, they do come to
express a kind of seeming dynamism through their matter
vestures. When those who are living in the matter outskirts of
the Palace of Truth, struggle hard to eke out their satisfaction
and happiness, fulfilling their desires, they too act invoking
their energy from the Spirit.

Even when the deluded ego-centres want to live in their realm of ignorance and sorrows, they need must invoke the required energy and sentience from the Pure Consciousness, the Self. Whether they seek their consolations in their moments of distress, or whether they are mere seekers of satisfaction for the demands of their body, for the urges of their mind, for the questions of their intellect, or whether they be mere men of desires, striving hard to fulfil their desires or to satisfy their emotions — they all need the energy to function, the capacity to feel and the ability to act. This dynamic motive power can reach the inert matter and vitalise it, only when the Spirit is invoked and contacted.

This invocation of the required type of energy to flow into a particular channel and act therein is called prayer *(Bhajan)*. In all true prayers the ego surrenders itself to the Spirit with a demand to its Lord to manifest and function in any given scheme of activity. As an analogy we may take the example of how we make use of an electric plug on the wall. The various equipments such as the fan or the heater or the toaster or the refrigerator — all are in themselves mere iron and steel mechanisms with no capacity of their own to perform work. Only when the electric current is flowing through them, can these gadgets serve the society.

If I plug into the wall a fan, it is an act where the fan is, as it were, invoking the dynamic current to flow through it. If the right instrument is contacted with the current, I will be served by the required manifestation. But supposing in winter I switch on the fan, I have no right then to complain that the electricity is cruel to me. If, unintelligently, I invoke the Truth to play through my mind which is mal-adjusted with wrong tendencies, the spirit flowing through such an instrument, can bring out nothing but sorrows for myself and disturbances to others.

With this scriptural idea, that the Self has the total monopoly of all sentience and life, Krishna here says that everyone — be he a sinner or a saint, foolish or wise, dull or energetic, cowardly or courageous — must invoke Me *(Bhajan)* and I express Myself through the individual mental composition as the one who has the above qualities. Each individual must approach Me, be it consciously or unconsciously, ere he can express himself at his intellectual or at his mental or at his physical personality.

If everyone must thus invoke the Self in expressing himself or in fulfilling his ideas and emotions, then everyone is "sacred" and "virtuous" for all without an exception are devotees at the Temple of the Spirit. Lord Krishna, the Self, now expounds, here in this stanza, how the numberless persons that reach him with endless prayers, can all be classified under four distinct groups.

(a) Men who are dissatisfied with even the best in life, approach this Life Energy in themselves, for fighting against and for gaining a total relief from the distress that is threatening them in their within.

(b) Seekers of knowledge and understanding in all fields of activities from mere idle curiosity to the difficult mathematical calculations, and subtle philosophical discussions, all of them ever invoke the grace of the Spirit.

(c) All men throughout their life time, spend themselves irresistibly in some field of activity, or the other under the whip of their own subjective desires. Fulfilment of desires is the urge under which every member of the living kingdom acts

restlessly all through his life time. The inert materials of the body and intellect cannot act unless the Spirit is invoked to play through them.

(d) We have yet a rare few, who approach the *sanctum sanctorum* of the Temple of the Spirit, demanding nothing, expecting nothing, carrying with them as their offerings only themselves. They offer themselves as an oblation in a pure spirit of love-inspired total self-surrender. The only cry in their heart is that the Spirit should end their sense of separation and accept them back to be embraced by the Lord, and made one with him. These *Gyanis* constitute the last of the types who try to invoke the Spirit.

Of these four types which is the best? ...

तेषां ज्ञानी नित्ययुक्त एकभक्तिर्विशिष्यते ।
प्रियो हि ज्ञानिनोऽत्यर्थमहं स च मम प्रियः ॥ १७ ॥

17. *tesham jnani nityayukta   ekabhaktir visisyate*
priyo hi jnanino 'tyartham   aham sa ca mama priyah

तेषाम् — Of them, ज्ञानी — the wise, नित्ययुक्तः — ever-steadfast, एकभक्तिः — whose devotion is to the one, विशिष्यते — excels, प्रियः — dear, हि — verily, ज्ञानिनः — of the wise, अत्यर्थम् — exceedingly, अहम् — I, सः — he, च — and, मम — of Me, प्रियः — dear.

17. *Of them the wise, ever steadfast and devoted to the One, excels, for, I am exceedingly dear to the wise, and he is dear to Me.*

Comparing and contrasting these four above-mentioned groups among themselves, the Lord declares here that the

Gyani, who, with a steadfast mind, surrenders himself to the Self with an integrated devotion, which is not dissipated by other parallel aspirations, represents the best. Single-pointedness of the mind can be gained only when the goal of the meditator is fixed and steady. The unbroken and all out aspiration of the seeker to reach his own real nature, the Self, is called single-pointed devotion *(Ekabhakti).*

This is possible only when one withdraws oneself, totally, from all other extroverted demands of the lower nature in him. In case of a *Gyani,* therefore, the Spirit is invoked not for the acquisition of anything, but for the annihilation of all the self destructive channels through which his spiritual dynamism gushes out day-to-day, to get wasted on the dry rocks of the world of his hallucination. Naturally, therefore, the Self, as a personification in Krishna, declares in Geeta that the *Gyanis* are the highest and the best, among the living kingdom, who reach the Portals of Truth with their individual demands and aspirations.

To the *Gyani "Supremely dear am I."* Love is measured by the amount of identification the lover has gained with beloved. Self-surrender is the tune in which the song of love is truly sung. Selflessness is the key in which the duet of love is played. Love demands "giving without expecting any return", at all times, in all circumstances. With this understanding of the nature of true love, when one tries to understand the attitude of the *Gyani* towards the Self, it is but true to say that, a *Gyani* alone knows how to love well and thoroughly.

One sided love never culminates in any consummation. Man may approach the Spiritual Centre in himself in an attitude of discrimination and surrender — with all his aspiration and love — but if it is not reciprocated by the Spirit, it might become as tragic as the Greek boy who fell in love with his own reflection. Here, when Krishna declares, *"and he is dear to Me"* a great psychological truth has been expounded. It is the Eternal Law of Love that love, with no strings attached to it, can not only order its own fulfilment but shall convert even the base into the noble by its silent persuasions and mysterious charms.

Scientifically viewed, it is an observable fact that if a mind, is powerfully charged with a certain emotion — may it be sorrow, hatred, jealousy, love or kindness — it can bring about sympathetic vibrations of similar emotions in the chambers of hearts that come near it. When one, full of hatred, approaches us, he can influence and fill our hearts to the full with hatred. So too, if we can give the required dose of pure and sincere love, unmotivated by any desire or selfishness, it is a law that even the bitterest enemies, with their full of hearts, can be forced to reflect nothing but love towards us. This psychological truth, in all its implications, has been brought out vividly when the Geeta states that even the Infinite and the Eternal Truth has to, helplessly, come under the charm of pure and selfless courting of the meditator with *Ekabhakti*.

Then, the three others, the distressed and the rest, are not dear to Vasudeva? Not so. Then how is it?

उदाराः सर्व एवैते ज्ञानी त्वात्मैव मे मतम् ।
आस्थितः स हि युक्तात्मा मामेवानुत्तमां गतिम् ॥ १८ ॥

18. *udarah sarva evai 'te   jnani tv atmai 'va me matam
    asthitah sa hi yuk tatma   mam eva 'nuttamam gatim*

उदाराः — Noble, सर्व — all, एव — surely, एते — these, ज्ञानी — the wise, तु — but, आत्मा — Self, एव — very, मे —

My, मतम् — opinion, आस्थितः — is established, सः — he,
हि — verily, युक्तात्मा — steadfast minded, माम् — Me, एव —
verily, अनुतमाम् — the Supreme, गतिम् — Goal.

18. *Noble indeed are all these; but the wise man, I deem,
as My very Self; for steadfast in mind he is established in me
alone as the Supreme Goal.*

With the large-heartedness of a master-mind, Lord
Krishna here declares that all creatures living the life of intelligent seeking and industrious efforts are blessed, inasmuch as
they are all, in their own way, approaching the same fountain
of the Infinite for tapping out their required energies.
Although some are invoking the Eternal Spiritual Strength
for the purpose of reducing their distress or for fulfilling their
desires, they are all, for one reason or the other, approaching
the Self, and therefore, relatively, they are diviner than the
insentient mineral world. However, comparing and contrasting them with the *Gyanis*, the Lord, says, *"But, the man of
Knowledge I regard as my own Self."*

It is very well-known that there is a lot of difference,
between one's friendship with the minister and oneself be-
coming a minister. No doubt to be a friend of a minister is to
gain some amount of influence and power in the society; but,
the entire might and glory come to the man when he himself
becomes the minister. Similarly, to be capable of invoking
and directing the Spiritual Strength is certainly divine, when
compared with the inert existence, wherein there is neither
the intellectual nor the mental capacities to live a conscious
life; but a man of Knowledge is one who, courting Truth in a
spirit of total identification with it, successfully attains the
total transcendence of his individual mind-and-intellect,

whereby his ego rediscovers itself to be nothing other than the Self. He becomes one with It.

Such a *Gyani,* thereafter, ever remains in the divine sense of identification with the Self. This emphasis of extra performance to the status of a man of wisdom, is, according to Krishna, his personal opinion *(Matam).* This term which is generally translated as religion is not a happy rendering. *Buddha Matam, Jaina Matam,* etc., means the opinion of those prophets and seers upon the eternal principles underlying all religions *(Dharma).* These opinions are generally changeable, when conditions and circumstances governing the era and influencing the age change. This subtle difference is generally overlooked in our hasty use of the term. Hindu *Dharma* declares the Eternal Principles upon which various prophets have given out their comments, from time to time, to bless their respective generations, who lived the conditions and circumstances then available to them in their peculiar ages.

बहूनां जन्मनामन्ते ज्ञानवान्मां प्रपद्यते ।
वासुदेवः सर्वमिति स महात्मा सुदुर्लभः ॥ १९ ॥

19. *bahunam janmanam ante   jnanavan mam prapadyate*
vasudevah sarvam iti   sa mahatma sudurlabhah

बहूनाम् — Of many, जन्मनाम् — of births, अन्ते — in the end, ज्ञानवान् — the wise, माम् — to Me, प्रपद्यते — approaches, वासुदेवः — Vasudeva, सर्वम् — all, इति — thus, सः — he, महात्मा — the great soul, सुदुर्लभः — (is) very hard to find.

19. *At the end of many births the wise man comes to Me, realising that all this is Vasudeva (the innermost Self); such a great soul* (Mahatma) *is very hard to find.*

That such pure men of wisdom are necessarily a rare few, in the history of the world, is the declaration here, which, in our decadent Hinduism, we have learnt to consider as an extremely pessimistic assertion.* A little thought should clearly make the fallacy in this wild conclusion quite evident to us. The entire human kingdom is, indeed, a very negligible and small proportion of the total sentient creatures in the world. Often, in the community of man, it is not all that have a fully developed instrument of rational thinking and divine emotions.

Even among those who have fully developed mental and intellectual capacities, it is a rare few that seriously take up the study of the scriptures. All those who study scriptures do not try to live the scriptures but they feel themselves fulfilled in a mere understanding of its contents. It, therefore, becomes evidently clear, that only a rare few can ever reach the goal of evolution and come to discover their true Divine Nature of Perfection.

Like Darwin in our own days, the ancient *Rishis* also have observed that this development can take place only, when, in the flood of time, the different circumstances have rubbed down and polished the imperfect into the shape and beauty of the perfect. It takes almost trillions of years for an organism to evolve from one given form of existence into another higher form of life. Naturally, it becomes quite clear that for a rational being of the subtlest potentialities as seen in man, it should take an indefinitely large number of lives in different manifestations to scrape off all his ignorance and thereby, ultimately reach the Perfect Realm of all Knowledge.

---

* Refer Discourse Chapter VI — 45.

This does not mean that no one among us, now striving so hard, as we do, at present, has any chance of reaching the goal of life in this very birth. It is not in any pessimistic hopelessness and total despair that this statement is made by the Lord in the Geeta. On the other hand, it is solely for bringing into the recognition of the student the urgency of his faithful pursuit of the higher life. The very fact that a seeker has come to feel a disappointment with his present state of existence, and the fact that he has discovered enough intellectual capacity to appreciate and comprehend the subtle thoughts of the Upanishadic lore, clearly shows that he has reached the very Arch-way to the Temple of the Self. A little more sincere and steady self-application can take him to the highest state of his evolution.

Now it will be shown why the people are not generally aware that the Self, or Vasudeva, alone is the all.

कामैस्तैस्तैर्हृतज्ञानाः प्रपद्यन्तेऽन्यदेवताः ।
तं तं नियममास्थाय प्रकृत्या नियताः स्वया ॥ २० ॥

20. *kamais tais-tair hrtajnanah   prapadyante 'nyadevatah*
   tam-tam niyamam asthaya   prakrtya niyatah svaya

कामैः — By desires, तैः तैः — by this or that, हृतज्ञानाः — those whose wisdom has been looted away, प्रपद्यन्ते — approach, अन्यदेवताः — other Gods, तं तम् — this or that, नियमम् — rite, आस्थाय — having followed, प्रकृत्या — by nature, नियताः — led, स्वया — by one's own.

20. *Those whose wisdom has been looted away by this or that desire, go to other Gods, following this or that rite, led by their own nature.*

Desire — for the sense-objects of the world and for sense gratification — is the one great cause from which the discriminative potentialities in the human intellect get constantly clouded. It is impossible that an individual is not made conscious of his own Self, in the light of a powerful and strong discrimination.

When the discriminative capacities are looted away, those deluded individuals, immediately, *"engage themselves in some ritualism or other, ordered by their nature, to propitiate one Devata or the other"*. Here, the entire stanza would yield almost no sense at all, if we follow only the dictionary-meaning of its words as the translators usually do. I do not mean that its word-meaning is incorrect; but, not forgetting that the Geeta is a universal scripture, when we read the stanza, we should expect Lord Krishna to discuss therein, a Truth, more Universal than merely a given religious faith. This attitude of our approach to the study of the Geeta is endorsed by Shri Murari himself, when he promises, in an earlier stanza* that he will be declaring to Arjuna not only the theoretical knowledge of the Vedic declaration *(Gyana)*, but also the practical experience *(Vigyana)* of its inner meaning.

Earlier, we were told that the deity for whose propitiation we performed the *Yagna*** was none other than "the productive potential in any given field of activity." Reading the stanza in the light of this interpretation, we may say that the deity mentioned here denotes nothing other than the various joys contained in the different sensuous fields which are courted by us, when we get ourselves lashed by desires, in

---

* VII — 2.
** Please refer Chapter 3 — the description of the 'Yagna-spirit' in which the Lord instructed the Karma Yogin to perform all his actions.

order that we may gain a complete and an exhaustive satisfaction from them.

Desires are the springs from which thoughts continuously gurgle up to flood the mental zone, and disturb the glorious reflection of the Truth in it. When the mind is thus disturbed the discriminative capacity in the intellect is rendered dull and naturally, that individual becomes incapable of distinguishing, in his understanding, the Real from the unreal. When thus, the brilliance of the human intellect has been clouded with the vapours of desire, the owls of negativity and delusory attachments start hooting in the jungles of that mind.

It is not the mere appearance of desires in the mind that causes the fall of man. No individual can resist the compelling charm of the desires rising in his bosom. But when he comes to identify himself with them, the thoughts rising in him are directly governed by his desires. When once a given desire has been identified with, the desirer himself, unconsciously, comes to lend an uncontrollable amount of dynamism to the upsurge of the flood of thoughts.

Thoughts themselves are inert matter, inasmuch as they are the by-products of food, being constituted of the subtlest aspect of the food consumed. These inert thought-waves gather a momentum and a force by borrowing their strength and vigour from the Self, through the individual's enthusiastic identification with those desires. The surge of thoughts determines the action. The actor in the field, for the time-being, is rendered incapable of discriminating whether the action undertaken can or cannot ultimately bring to him a permanent and an enduring satisfaction. Drunk with the idea that he will be able to gain at least a temporary appeasement, the individual struggles hard and strives intensively to invoke and propitiate *"the productive potential of any given fields of his activity" (Devata)*.

In thus invoking the *Devata* of a given field, the individual has to strive in a proper and fitting fashion. The methods of assembling the required instruments, the techniques of their application, the time intervals necessary for maturing the results, and the type of gains accrued from the different kinds of application . . . all these differ from field to field in the world. Therefore, each one will have to *"follow this or that rite,"* according to the type of his desires.

The reason why different persons thus struggle hard so differently, leaving aside all sincere struggles to realise the Self, as *"Vasudeva is these all"*, is explained here in the second line. Each individual helplessly functions in the different fields of his temporary fascinations, according to his mental impressions, gathered in his earlier moments of activity and thought. To conceive that 'the Creator is putting ideas into each one of us because of which one is good and another vile,' is a philosophy of the defeatist, of the impotent, of the sluggard. The true men of action, with the daring of a well-developed intellect, can very easily see through men and their behaviours and come to this bold conclusion that each man acts as per the schedule, maintained and ordered by himself, during his own past actions.

In short, a deluded person strives hard, running after the mirage of sensuality, hoping to gain therein, a satisfaction that is at once infinite and immortal, while another is found to have the subtle vision to discriminate and discover for himself, the hollowness and futility of the sense-pursuit. This latter type withdraws from all these ultimately unprofitable fields, and with avidity seeks — the Path to the Real.

What then is the function of the Atman, the guardian angel in each one of us?

यो यो यां यां तनुं भक्तः श्रद्धयार्चितुमिच्छति ।
तस्य तस्याचलां श्रद्धां तामेव विदधाम्यहम् ॥ २१ ॥

21. *yo-yo yam-yam tanum bhaktah*
     sraddhaya 'rcitum icchati
     tasya-tasya calam sraddham
     tam eva vidahamy aham

यः — Who, यः — who, याम् — which, याम् — which, तनुम् — form, भक्तः — devotee, श्रद्धया — with faith, अर्चितुम् — to worship, इच्छति — desires, तस्य — of him, तस्य — of him, अचलाम् — unflinching, श्रद्धाम् — faith, ताम् — that, एव — surely, विदधामि– make, अहम् — I.

21. *Whatsoever form any devotee desires to worship with faith — that (same) faith of his I make (firm and) unflinching.*

No other scriptural text-book, existing in the world to-day can be truly considered as an Universal Scripture, as we can rightly consider the Divine Song of the Lord of Brinda-van. When religions are built upon the limited declarations of great prophets, given out by them during their mortal exist-ence in this ever-changing world, they naturally, have the knack of turning out fanatics; without blind faith in their Prophets, the Bibles of the world cannot, for a moment, hold within their embrace the entire mass of their 'faithful follow-ers'. Love for one Prophet, when whipped up beyond a cer-tain tempo, must encourage an intolerance with every other prophet!

When personalities are worshipped and followed, rather

than the ideas preached and the idealisms lived by them, it almost always results in breeding fanatics. Even among the Hindus when they come to worship as devotees of one or the other of the *Pauranic*-Gods, they too split up into opposing camps of *Vaishnavites* and *Saivites,* and shamelessly fight among themselves, as political parties do, in their excitement during the election campaigns.

Vedanta respects no personalities; no personality is considered as all important in Vedanta. It is a text-book, enunciating and proving the Science or Right Living, and as such, the *Rishis* are but the mouth-pieces that declare the *Rishi*-experiences. As a faithful interpreter of the Science of Vedanta, whenever Geeta comes to declare the application of that Science in life, it immediately rises to the full stature of a Scripture of Man from a mere religious text-book of the Hindu *Vaishnavites*. The stanzas under review, provide us with a set of excellent examples proving the universality of the Divine Song.

In the very opening of this chapter, discriminating the Self from the not-Self, it was shown how Krishna is the Spiritual Principal, the Common Truth that holds together the mutliple universe of names and forms.* It was also said** that the three-fold mental temperaments *(Gunas),* that work up the divine illusion, hoodwink the individual from the right cognition of the Divine Self in him. But for the Conscious Principle thrilling the inert matter walls that seemingly encircle the spirit, neither our physical nor the mental nor the intellectual personalities can ever come to function, as they do. It is very well known, that all men do not worship at the

---

* VII — 7.
** *Ibid* 41.

same altar. Each one approaches the same Truth by worship-
ping the idol of his own heart. Krishna here declares the
Sacred Truth that in all Churches, Mosques, and Temples, in
public places or in private institutions, in the open or on the
sly, in the quiet huts and in the silent caves — wherever and
whatsoever form any devotee seeks to worship *with Sraddha*
"his faith do I make unwavering". A faithful follower of the
Geeta can never be contaminated by sectarianism or intolerance. At the foot of every altar, it is Krishna, the Self, that
constantly supplies more and more faith to water the expand-
ing fields of devotion in the sincere devotees.

Applying this general statement to the subjective worship in the human bosom, we can very easily understand the
greater imports of this stanza.

In the world outside, it is very well known that the greater
the consistency with which an idea or an attachment is maintained by an individual, the greater does he become fixed in
that temperament or relationship. The more often a particular type of thought is entertained in the mind, the deeper
becomes that thought-channel, strengthening that very mental impression. These deep-cut patterns of thought, ploughed
along the valleys of the mind, indicate the pattern of desires
which the individual entertained. In the law that governs this
psychological rule, we can spy and detect the Spiritual Reality
and Its infinite and glorious might.

In short, the Lord says that "as we think so we become",
and the more we become, the more we think in the same given
pattern. Applying this principle of Psychology, it becomes
clear beyond all doubts, why everyone of us is bound by our
own habits and how we get chained up by our own peculiar
type of thinking. The sensuous is not to be condemned, and

equally so, the divine need not be congratulated. Both of them are the exact products of their individual types of thinking. Thought belongs to the realm of Nature *(Prakriti);* thoughts create the world and the All-pervading Self is the essential Substratum *(Purusha)* that provides the world-drama with its stage and scenario.

With this ever-growing faith, how does the man-of-the-world gain his particular desires?

स तया श्रद्धया युक्तस्तस्याराधनमीहते ।
लभते च ततः कामान्मयैव विहितान्हि तान् ॥ २२ ॥

22.　*sa taya sraddhaya yuktas　tasya 'radhanam ihate
labhate ca tatah kaman　mayai 'va vihitan hi tan*

सः — He, तया — with that, श्रद्धया — with faith, युक्तः — endued, तस्य — of it, आराधनम् — worship, ईहते — engage in, लभते — obtains, च — and, ततः — from that, कामान् — desires, मया — by Me, एव — surely, विहितान् — ordained, हि — verily, तान् — those.

22. *Endued with that faith, he engages in the worship of that* (Devata) *and from it he obtains his desire : all these being ordained, indeed, by Me (alone).*

Imbued with this faith he invokes the *Devata* of his choice and gains his desires. And, Lord Krishna adds that in all cases these desires are *"being verily dispensed by Me alone"*. The Self is the source of all activities, gains, fulfilments and despairs. The sense of joy or sorrow, of success or failure, is but a mental thought-wave; but for the Conscious Principle illumining it, we would not be aware of any such experience.

Faithful activity in any given field of action, brings about complete success but the very existence of the field, the capacity to act, the fervour of faith that supplies consistency to all efforts — all these are possible only in the medium of the Changeless, the Actionless, the Attributeless Self Eternal. And Krishna, identifying Himself with this Spiritual Centre of the Universe, rightly declares here, that He alone is the one that supplies an ever growing faith in all activities and ultimately, when the laws of action are fulfilled to the last bit, both in their intensity and application, it is He alone who dispenses the exact result for each action.

When a well-adjusted radio is plugged on to the current, the Electric Current says that it alone is the 'dispenser' of the programme available at the Station for the listeners.

Since the deluded ones desire the finite sense objects, they do not come to the all-satisfying peace and hence, it is said:—

अन्तवतु फलं तेषां तद्भवत्यल्पमेधसाम् ।
देवान्देवयजो यान्ति मद्भक्ता यान्ति मामपि ॥ २३ ॥

23. *antavat tu phalam tesam   tad bhavaty alpamedhasam*
     devam devayajo yanti   madbhakta yanti mam api

अन्तवत् — Finite, तु — verily, फलम् — the fruit, तेषाम् — of them, तद् — that, भवति — is, अल्पमेधसाम्— those of small intelligence, देवान्— to the Gods, देवयज: — the worshippers of the Devas, यान्ति — go to, मद्भक्ता:- My devotees, यान्ति — go to, माम् — to Me, अपि — also.

23. *Verily the fruit that accrues to those men of little intelligence is finite. The worshippers of the Devas go to the Devas, but My devotees come to Me.*

The fruits accruing to *"these men of little understanding are limited"*. Fleeting desires for finite objects, even when fulfilled through the impermanent activities, must surely prove themselves to be ephemeral. Out of gold whatever ornament is made, it also must be gold alone; when chocolate is made out of sweet things, the resultant stuff cannot be bitter. The effects entirely depend, for their nature and quality, upon those of the causes.

Finite actions undertaken in finite fields, employing finite instruments, cannot but produce, — whether joy or sorrow — finite fruits. Joy arrested or ended is sorrow; and, therefore, in each instance of a sensuous desire satisfied, though there is a joy and a fulfilment, the sense-of-satisfaction soon putrefies to provide the sourness of dissatisfaction, or, more often, the bitterness of sorrow.

This statement of the Lord is supported by the following general rule that, *"the worshippers of the Devas reach the Devas"*. Those who are invoking a desired 'potential profit' in any given field of activity can, even when completely successful, gain only *that* profit.

The above statement is declared as a contrast to a pure philosophical truth, when the Lord says: *"those who devote themselves to Me, come to Me"* Seekers of happiness in the world of sense-objects, as a result of their strife and struggle, can gain their insignificant success in the fields of sense-enjoyments. If the same effort is applied by them in the right life of constructive living, they can come to discover their identity with the Eternal Absolute, the Self. Due to the extro-version of the deluded Ego, it comes to identity itself with its finite matter envelopments and reveal itself in a world of its objects, called in Sanskrit as the *Jagat*.

Discriminative and careful seekers, understanding the utter uselessness of the pursuit of the finite pleasures, detach themselves from their false ego-centric lives and through the process of meditation upon the Self, as advised in the previous chapter, come to rediscover their own Real Nature in the sunny fields of Bliss that lie unrolled beyond the thorny by-lanes of the physical, the psychological and the intellectual quests.

In the language of the Geeta, the first person singular always at all places, stands for the Infinite Reality which is the Substratum, for the individual, as well as for the Whole. Therefore, *"My devotees come to Me"* is not the assertion of a limited historical figure as the son of Devaki, but the Singer of the Geeta, in His divine inspiration, entirely identifies Himself with the Principle of Consciousness that is the core of the pluralistic dream of the mind-intellect equipment. Thus, to understand the above statement, without its seeming limitations, is to understand the Geeta, the Scripture of Man, as declaring that the seekers of the Self discover themselves and become the Self.

"Then why do people in general fail to reach the Self?" *Listen:*—

अव्यक्तं व्यक्तिमापन्नं मन्यन्ते मामबुद्धयः ।
परं भावमजानन्तो ममाव्ययमनुत्तमम् ॥ २४ ॥

24.   *avyaktam vyaktim apannam*
       manyante mam 'abuddhayah
       param bhavam ajananto
       mama 'vyayam anuttamam

अव्यक्तम् — The Unmanifested, व्यक्तिम्— to manifesta-

tion, आपन्नम्— come to, मन्यन्ते— think, माम्— Me, अबुद्धयः—
the foolish, परम्— the highest, भावम् — nature, अजानन्तः —
not knowing, मम — My, अव्ययम् — immutable, अनुत्तमम् —
most excellent.

24. *The foolish think of Me, the Unmanifest, as having
come to manifestation, not knowing My higher, immutable
and peerless nature.*

Men who lack discrimination and the capacity to perceive
the subtle Truth, that shines in and through the vast disturbances of the endless plurality, fail to realise the immutable and
the peerless Self. In their extreme preoccupation with the
everchanging glory of the perceivable, the *Prakriti,** they do
not understand that *"all this is strung on Me as a row of jewels
on a thread."***

This fundamental Reality, that is the beam of brilliance
in which like dust-particles the Universes dance about, is
termed as the "Unmanifest." This term is to be understood in
all its philosophical implications. That which is called the
manifest is available either for the perceptions of the sense-
organs, or for the feelings of the mind, or for the understanding of the intellect. That which is not available for any one of
these instruments of cognition, feeling or understanding, is
considered as the *Unmanifest*.

The Self, indeed, should then be considered as the *Unmanifest*, for it is the Vitality behind the sense-organs, the
Feeler-potential in the mind, and the very Light that illumines
the intellect.***

* VII—4 and 5.
** *Ibid* 7
*** Refer Swamiji's "Discourses on Kanopanishad".

The distorted intellects of the extroverts, in their mis-calculations, come to the false judgement that the physical glory of the Prophet or the incarnation is all that is the Eternal Truth. The Point-of-Concentration *(Upasya)* is to be con-sidered, no doubt, as the symbol of Truth which the devotee is seeking, but it cannot be in itself the Truth. If it were the Truth, then after carving out an idol or after approaching a Guru, the devotee has nothing more to do, since he has gained the Truth. Idol worship is only a convenience for the true seekers, so that they may gain during moments of their devoted concentration, a momentum, for the final fight, into themselves, to reach the Self and discover their own oneness with It.

Vyasa, as the father of 'form-worship', through his im-mortal works, the *Puranas,* had perhaps, in his infinite wis-dom felt, that in the long run, the intellectually dull devotees, in their mad emotionalism, might come to mistake the means for the end. In order to remove this danger, the great Saint is making the Lord himself declare here that *"the foolish regard Me, the Unmanifested, as having come to manifestation."*

The fears of the great Seer have come true in our own days!* If only they would listen to their own Lord, himself disowning here what they, the ignorant devotees, blindly believe in their utter superstition. It will do them no harm if they remember, at least now and then, that the Geeta is not a text-book dedicated to some special "hard hearted intellects, living the life of the caves" — as the glorious *Rishis* are being condemned by those who can never understand the Seers of the Upanishads.

---

* Even when this pen is writing these lines the writer has to resist his pen, for already some wise-looking mis-guided devotees have taken their cudgels against this commentator, to hoot in the dark valleys of their prejudices, ominous threats, that as a Vedantin, he is against idol-worship.

This stanza gives us a clear insight into the futility of mistaking the bottle for the medicine, the physical form for the Guru, the idol for the God. All white wood is not the fragrant sandalwood. Any bright light high up in the sky, however resplendent it might be, is not the Sun. Because some blind men of incomparable foolishness declare that the light from a tower is the Sun no wise man of the town can accept it. The idea of Divine Incarnation is accepted in Hinduism and according to its theory everyone is an incarnation to a degree. The same Truth pervades all, and in each. It expresses through the enveloping layers of mind-and-intellect. The clearer the mind and the purer the intellect the greater is the effulgence of the Divine that beams out of them.

When the Self in anyone happens to beam out through the steadied and purified mind and intellect and thus his lower nature *(Prakriti)* is almost completely sublimated, he becomes a Prophet, a Sage. Krishna, Rama, Christ, Allah, Buddha, Mahavir are, some of the examples. These men of Realisation discovering their Self, understood and lived every moment of their lives in the Self, as the Self of all. To mistake the physical structure or the lingering traces of their mind, or the film of their intellectual personality for the very Essence of truth, which these God-men were, is to make as miserable a mistake as taking the waves to be the ocean.

Naturally, therefore, Krishna uses here a severe term for such deluded men of superstitious false understanding as the *"unintelligent fools"*.

What causes this prevalent ignorance of the True Nature is explained in the following :—

नाहं प्रकाशः सर्वस्य योगमायासमावृतः ।
मूढोऽयं नाभिजानाति लोको मामजमव्ययम् ॥ २५ ॥

25. *na 'ham prakasah sarvasya   yogamayasamavritah*
     mudho 'yam na 'bhijanati   loko mam ajam avyayam

न — Not, अहम् — I, प्रकाशः — manifest, सर्वस्य — of all,
योगमायासमावृतः — veiled by divine Maya, मूढः — deluded,
अयम् — this, न — not, अभिजानाति — knows, लोकः — world,
माम् — Me, अजम् — Unborn, अव्ययम् — Imperishable.

25. *I am not manifest to all (in My Real Nature) veiled by*
Divine-Maya. *This deluded world knows not Me, the Unborn,*
the Imperishable.

If there be such a glorious Essential Truth Factor, which
is the Core of everything, why is it that it is not freely known
and experienced by everyone at all times? In short, "what
stands between me and myself?" Why is it that we behave as
though we are but the limited Ego-centres not even able to
comprehend that in the essence we are the Infinite, the
Immortal? These questions are unavoidable to an intelligent
seeker when he, in his aspirations, comes face to face with the
staggering revelations contained in Vedanta.

"*This deluded world knows Me not, the Unborn and*
immortal," because their own "*illusion, born out of the three*
Gunas, veils Me" from them. *Maya* is the most difficult theme
of all for all elementary students of Vedanta, when they try
merely to understand objectively, this Science of Life. The
moment a student tries to experiment this knowledge upon
himself subjectively, the explanations contained in the theory
become evident. *Maya* is the conditioning, through which,
when the Non-dual Truth expresses Itself, the One Reality
seems to fan out as the spectrum of the multiple universe.

The principle of *Maya* functioning in the individual, is termed ignorance *(Avidya).* This subjective malady, which provides in its wake, the dreamy hallucinations of a sorrowful world of change and imperfections, has been very closely observed, and the Rishis of old have declared that it is caused by three types of 'germs' in man's inner personality. These three temperaments *(gunas),* called *Sattwa, Rajas* and *Tamas,* provide a prism, viewed through which, the Kaleidoscopic world seems to dance, parading its infinite patterns, *Rajas* creates "mental agitations," *(Vikshepa)* and *Tamas* creates "intellectual veiling" *(Avarana).**

By the play of these triple temperaments, when one becomes confused and confounded, to him the Self is not available for direct experience. Special instructions from teachers and diligent practice on the part of students are both necessary in order to make one realise one's own Real Nature. To an ignorant man of the jungle, electricity is unmanifest in the bulb and in its efflorescent filament. In order to perceive the electrical current that flows through the equipment, theoretical knowledge and experimental confirmation are unavoidable. After having gained the knowledge of electrical energy and its properties, when the student happens to see the very same bulb, he comes to cognise through the perceived bulb the imperceptible, and therefore, the unmanifest, electrical energy.

Similarly, when through self-control, listening, reflection and meditation, the agitations of the mind are controlled and quietened and when the veiling has thus been pulled down, the seeker rediscovers *"Me, the Unborn, the Immutable".* As

---

* Refer "Fall and Rise of Man" in Swamiji's *"Discourses on Kenopanishad".*

long as the agitations of the mind veil the intellect from its awareness of the Self, so long the limited ego, pants to fulfil itself and to gain the Infinite among the gutters of its sensual cravings!

Such frenzied hearts reeking with desires and lacerated with disappointments, crushed by dissatisfactions and smothered by the fear of their own annihilation — can never have the integrated equipoise to live, at least, a moment of still-awareness to experience the Pure Consciousness. *"The deluded world knows Me not"* as they are steeped in *"the illusion born out of the three-fold gunas"*. Screened off by this universe of names and forms, which is but an apparent projection of the Self, the ordinary sense-organs, mind or intellect fail to preceive it. The ghost veils the post; the mirage-waters clothe the desert; the waves screen off the ocean!!

The present condition of ignorance and confusion in the limited finite Ego is brought out very vividly in the following, by contrasting it against the background of the Self, which is of the Nature of All-Knowledge :—

वेदाहं समतीतानि वर्तमानानि चार्जुन ।
भविष्याणि च भूतानि मां तु वेद न कश्चन ॥ २६ ॥

26. *veda 'ham samatitani   vartamanani ca 'rjuna*
    bhavisyani ca bhuttani   mam tu veda na kascana

वेद — Know, अहम् — I, समतीतानि— the past, वर्तमानानि— the present, च — and, अर्जुन — O Arjuna, भविष्याणि— the future, च — and, भूतानि — beings, माम् –- Me, तु —verily, वेद — knows, न — not, कश्चन — any one.

26. *I know, O Arjuna, the beings of the past, and present and the future, but no one knows Me.*

The idea that God is Omniscient, is common to all religions of the world, but a satisfactory explanation of this concept is given only in Vedanta. In Geeta too — as a Bible of the religion, as a hand-book of easy reference for the students of the Upanishads — we find a mere hint as to the Omniscience of the Self.

The Self, as the Pure Consciousness, is the illuminating principle that brings the entire field of the mind and intellect under the beam of our clear awareness. Even the world-of-objects is brought within our understanding only when it enters, through the sense-organ-doors, to reach the mental lake and make therein its characteristic thought-waves; the thought-waves make the intellect function in classifying and determining the objects. Both these mental and intellectual disturbances are illuminated for us by the ever wakeful Consciousness, the Self in us.

The Self is the same everywhere. In all bosoms it is the same Conscious Principle that illuminates their respective thoughts and ideas. Naturally, therefore, the Self represents the Awareness that illumines or knows, all thoughts and ideas in every living organism.

The sun-light illuminates all objects of the world. When my eyes or ears illumine a given form or sound, I say that I see or hear that particular form or sound; in short, to be aware of a thing is to know that thing; and to know is to illumine. Just as the sun can be considered as the "Eye of the world," inasmuch as without the Sun all organs of vision will be blind apertures, so too, the Self can be considered as the Knower of every-thing, in everyone, at all times, and in all places. This Omniscience of the Supreme is vividly hinted at here, when Krishna declares, *"I know the beings of the past, of the present and of the future"*.

It must be noted that the Eternal Self is not only the Awareness that lights up all bosoms at this present moment, but it *was* the Awareness that illuminated the objects, feelings and thoughts in all bosoms from the beginningless beginning of creation and it *shall* be the same Principle behind every knower that knows anything in all the future generations till the endless end of time.

Electricity revolves the fan; but the fan can never fan the electricity! The gazer surveys the heavens through a telescope, but the telescope can never survey the gazer! The Conscious Principle vitalises the food-made mind and intellect and makes them capable of feeling and thinking. Without the Self dynamising them, they are incapable of sense-perceptions; but neither the mind nor the intellect can perceive, feel or comprehend the Subjective Principle, the Self. The Lord declares here that though he knows everything, at all times, in all places, he is known by none at any place or at any time — *"But Me none knows"*.

According to the strictest Vedantic philosophy, the Self is not a knower, just as in the strictest logic of thought it would not be correct to say that the sun illumines the world. From our standpoint, contrasting with the hours of night when things are not illumined, we may rightly attribute the function of illuminating things during the day to the 'principle of light' called the sun. However, from the standpoint of the sun, which is ever brilliant, there is no moment when he is not blessing the objects with his shining touch. Therefore, it is as meaningless to say that the sun illumines the objects, as to say that "I am too busy now-a-days breathing!"

The 'knower-hood' is a status that is gained by the Self when It functions through the equipment of *Maya;* and the

Self, that functions in and through the delusory *Maya** is called the God-Principle, termed in the Vedantic literature as *Iswara*. Krishna here is pictured by Vyasa as the divine embodiment of Truth and Incarnation of the Self, and therefore, it is perfectly right if he arrogates to Himself the nature of omnisciency and declares Himself as *"the knower of everything, in all the three periods of time"*.

But, unfortunately, an Ego-centric mortal, viewing the universe through the pin-hole of his congested, constricted and limited mind-and-intellect, fails to see the harmonious rhythm in the macrocosm. He who can rip open his own self-made bondages of ignorance and rise to attune himself with the macrocosm, can certainly come to experience the Krishna view-point. Anyone who successfully comes to live thus in unison with the cosmic mind, is the Krishna of that age and for ever thereafter.

"If the Self is the Eternal Knower of all conditioned-Knowledge, then what veils this Essential Nature from our realisation of the same?" Listen :—

इच्छाद्वेषसमुत्थेन द्वंद्वमोहेन भारत ।
सर्वभूतानि संमोहं सर्गे यान्ति परंतप ॥ २७ ॥

27. *icchadvesasamutthena   dvandvamohena bharata*
     sarvabhutani sammoham   sarge yanti parantapa

इच्छाद्वेषसमुत्थेन — Arisen from desire and aversion, द्वन्द्व-मोहेन— by the delusion of the pairs-of-opposites, भारत — O Bharata, सर्वभूतानि— all beings, संमोहम् — to delusion, सर्गे — at birth, यान्ति — are subject, परन्तप— O Parantapa.

---

* The congress of the three gunas wherein Sattwa predominates the other two — *Sattvaguna-pradhana Mayo-pahita, Brahman, Iswarah,* — is Lord the Eswara.

27. By the delusion of the pairs-of-opposites arising from desire and aversion, O Bharata, all beings are subject to delusion at birth, O Parantapa (scorcher of foes).

A highly scientific and extremely subtle philosophical truth has been suggested in this stanza. In his attempt to explain why and how the ego-centric personality in man fails to cognise his all-full nature the Lord touches, by implication, the very fundamentals discovered and discussed by the modern biologists in explaining the evolution of organisms. The instinct of self-preservation is the most powerful urge under which the individualised-ego tries to live its life of continuous change. This instinct of preservation expresses itself, in the intellectual zone, as binding desires for things that contribute to the continuous welfare and well-being of the individual's mundane existence.

When the impulse of desire, flowing from a bosom towards an object of attachment, gets bumped half-way upon an object or a being that stands between the bosom that craves and the object-of-craving, the refracted desire-thoughts express themselves as aversion.* In the tug-of-war between these two forces of desire and aversion, the helpless ego gets torn asunder and comes to suffer the agonising pain of lynching tensions. Naturally, its mind-and-intellect becomes fully pre-occupied with its pursuits after things of its desire and with its efforts at running away from the objects of its aversion. Soon the ego-centric personality becomes endlessly pre-occupied, totally confused and completely exhausted. The host of thought-disturbances that are thereby created in the mental and in the intellectual zones, breed among themselves and add day by day to the chaos within. This 'agitation'

---

* Refer Chapter II, 62 and 63.

(Vikshepa) is that which veils *(Avarana)* the Truth from the direct cognition of the individual. Therefore, the only way by which we can come to rediscover our equipoise and tranquillity, as the Eternal Self, is to arrest, control and win over the agitations of the mind. All spiritual practices in all religions of the world are techniques — either emotional, or intellectual or physical — that aim at bringing about at least one solitary moment of perfect mental poise. Such a moment of poise is the moment of perfect mental illumination, the auspicious hour of rediscovery and fulfilment of the re-union.

But unfortunately, adds the Lord in a divinely pathetic note, that *"all beings fall into this delusion at their very birth"*. This is not a pessimistic submission as to the sorrowful destiny of man, from which he is from birth incapacitated to escape. Unlike the Christ-religion, our Krishna-religion does not conceive of man as a child of sin. The Master optimist, the Teacher of Hope, the Joyous Dancer of the Jamuna-banks, is here expressing only a philosophical truth, that the very birth of an individual into a given embodiment, with its available environment, is the tragedy that he himself had planned out elaborately for the fulfilment of his own deep cravings and secret desires.

To get out of this delusion and gain the right knowledge is the Sacred Goal of Life and the Geeta is the Song of the Self that enchants the erring souls away from their confusions to the soft fields of the joyous Perfection.

To show then what are the qualifications of those who seek the Truth, the following is given :—

येषां त्वन्तगतं पापं जनानां पुण्यकर्मणाम् ।
ते द्वंद्व मोहनिर्मुक्ता भजन्ते मां दृढव्रताः ॥ २८ ॥

28. *yesam tu antagatam papam   jananam punyakarmanam*
      te dvandvamohanirmukta   bhajante mam dradhavratah

येषाम् — Of whom, तु — but, अन्तगतम् — is at an end,
पापम् — sin, जनानाम् — of men, पुण्यकर्मणाम् — of virtuous
deeds, ते — they, द्वन्द्व–मोहनिर्मुक्ताः — freed from the delusion
of the pairs of opposites, भजन्ते— worship, माम्— Me, दृढव्रताः:-
men steadfast in vows.

28. *But those men of virtuous deeds whose sins have come
to an end, who are freed from the delusion of the pairs-of-
opposites and are steadfast in vows, worship Me.*

"*Men of virtuous deeds,*" as a result of their actions,
"*come to cleanse all their sinful nature*" is a declaration that
needs to be rightly understood. Sin is not the nature of man;
according to Vedanta, it is only the tarnish that has come to
dim the brilliance of the Self, due to an error of judgement in
the individual. The craving of the mind-and-intellect, to live
in subservience to the calls and appetites of the grosser outer
world, is the root-cause for the negative values entertained by
us, which ultimately result in 'sins.' He is called a sinful-
person in whom, his body makes the heartiest calls on his time
and attention. In such a person, the body becomes the domi-
nant partner, 'enslaves' the Self. The extrovert life — a life
spent in pursuing the satisfaction of sensuous desires, in the
consolation of every paltry emotion, and the fulfilment of
each wayward desire — is the way of the sinful.

Such a passionate animal-life leaves gross impressions
upon the mind and intellect. Impressions *(Vasanas)* decide
the future flow of thoughts. As the thoughts, so the actions.
And the action deepens the *Vasanas!*

To break this '*Vasana-thought-action*' chain, which is

now digging the grave of the individual's peace and tranquillity, it is advised that he start a new line of meritorious actions. Merit *(punya)* is a contrast to sin *(papa)* and therefore, it is constituted of actions, feelings, and thoughts, dedicated to the godly and the divine. All introvert actions undertaken in the recognition of *"the Self I am,"* would create in their wake new impressions. In the long run, the patterns of sin that existed in the bosom are wiped out and the new divine designs are created therein.

Such a prepared mind-intellect, from which almost all its negatives have been rubbed off is *"freed from the delusion of the pairs-of-opposites"*. It then becomes an instrument that can, with a single-pointed steadfastness and firm resolve, meditate upon the Self.

What would be the motive in the heart of those who are thus meditating upon the Self, after their minds have been re-adjusted by living the life-divine?

जरामरणमोक्षाय मामाश्रित्य यतन्ति ये ।
ते ब्रह्म तद्विदुः कृत्स्नमध्यात्मं कर्म चाखिलम् ॥ २९ ॥

29. *jaramaranamoksaya   mam asritya yatantiye*
te brahma tad viduh krtsnam
adhyaatman Karma cu 'khilam

जरामरणमोक्षाय — For liberation from old age and death, माम् — Me, आश्रित्य — having taken refuge in, यतन्ति — strive, ये — who, ते — they, ब्रह्म — Brahman, तत् — that, विदुः — know, कृत्स्नम् — the whole, अध्यात्मम् — knowledge of the Self, कर्म — action, च — and अखिलम् — whole.

29. *Those who strive for liberation from old age and*

death, taking refuge in Me, — they realise in full that Brahman,
the whole knowledge of the Self and all action.

Those who thus strive diligently to cleanse their hearts of
their wrong tendencies and bring their minds so purified for
the higher contemplation of the Self, do so in order to gain,
"the freedom from old age and *death*". But the modern world
is also striving to discover methods of arresting death and
avoiding old age. However, this physical continuity of existence in the world is not the goal that has been hinted at here in
the Science of Spiritual Evolution.

Birth, growth, disease, decay and death, are the natural
modifications that should come into the person of every man
or being that continues in a given manifestation to the ripe old
age of its full existence. Such modification, as an experience
of change is the agonising source of pains. But for this change,
a complete and unbroken happiness would be our lot. The
attempt of a spiritual seeker in his meditation upon the Self is
to get over all his identifications with the realm of change, and
the entire province of change is indicated by these two familiar
terms *"old age and death"*.

Such a true meditator, meditating upon the Self, comes
to realise his identity with the Conscious Principle in him, the
Self. The Self in the individual *(Atman)* is the Eternal Truth,
which is the Substratum for the whole universe *(Brahman)*.
To realise the Self is to become the Brahman, since, the Self in
the individual is the One Self everywhere. This non-duality of
the Truth is implied here in this stanza when it declares that
those who meditate upon Me, the Self, come to *"know the*
Brahman".

When an ordinary man of the world, intelligent and
sincere though he might be, comes to read and understand

Vedanta, he is apt to come to the hasty conclusion that the realisation of the *Brahman* is, indeed, a glorious achievement, but that it has nothing to do with the life, in the world thereafter. It is the general misconception in Hinduism, that the religious man must leave the world and live in a strange realm of his own, self-exiled from the destinies of joys and sorrows, problems and achievements, failures and successes of the Society in which he lives!!

This dire misconception has thrown more slur upon our culture than anything else. That the man of realisation is not thereafter an impotent fool in the worldly transactions has been clearly brought out here, when Krishna says that the Perfected One, not only realises the All-Pervading Self, but at once comprehends *"the working of the psychological forces (Adhyatma) in him and becomes proficient in all activities (Karma)"*. It is very well realised by all men of experience that he alone can serve the world who has a full and complete knowledge of the psychology of the world and has also a perfect control over his own mind. A man of harmonious Perfection is the fittest instrument to sing the Song of Truth and such an individual must be the best integrated personality, smart and efficient in all activities.

Continuing the same idea and expressing how a man of wisdom is a man of all-knowledges and all efficiency, Krishna declares :—

साधिभूताधिदैवं मां साधियज्ञं च ये विदुः ।
प्रयाणकालेऽपि च मां ते विदुर्युक्तचेतसः ॥ ३० ॥

30.   *sadhibhutadhidaivam mam   sadhiyajnam ca ye viduh*
      prayanakale 'pi ca mam   te vidur yuktacetasah

साधिभूताधिदैवम् — With the *Adhibhuta*, with the
Adhidaiva together, माम् — Me, साधियज्ञम् — with the *Adhiyajna*, च — and, ये — who, विदुः — know, प्रयाणकाले — at the
time of death, अपि — even, च — and, माम् — Me, ते — they,
विदुः — know, युक्तचेतसः — steadfast in mind.

30. *Those who know Me with the* Adhibhuta *(pertaining
to elements, the world of objects),* Adhidaiva *(pertaining to the
Gods, the sense-organs) and the* Adhiyajna *(pertaining to the
sacrifice, all perceptions), even at the time of death, steadfast in
mind know Me.*

Not only that the man of realisation understands all the
vagaries of the mind and the nature of all activities, but he also
gains a perfect knowledge of the world-of-objects *(Adhibhuta)*, the secrets behind the workings of the sense-organs,
mind and intellect *(Adhidaiva)*, and the conditions under
which all perceptions — physical, mental and intellectual —
(Adhiyajna), can best take place.

The common idea that a man of God is an impractical
man inefficient to live a successful life in the world, may be
true as far as a dedicated devotee of a particular God-form or
a Prophet is concerned. The *Upasaka* is one who is so fully
engrossed with his emotions and thoughts, dedicated to the
Lord of his heart, that he has neither the interest nor the
capacity to know the ways of the world. But the Man of
Perfection, as conceived by the Science of Vedanta, is not
only a man of perfection in the realm of the Spirit, but he is
also, at all times, on all occasions, under all situations, a
master of himself and a dynamic force to be reckoned with.

He essentially becomes the leader of the world, as he is
master of his own mind, as well as the minds of the entire

living kingdom. To him, thereafter, everything becomes clear, and such a Man of Perfection lives in the world as a God in his Knowledge of the worlds, both within and without.

In short, the chapter closes with a total assertion that, *"he who knows Me knows everything"*, and he is a man who will come to guide the destinies of the world, not only in his own times, but in the days to come, as Lord Krishna himself did.

These two closing stanzas of this chapter do not of themselves explain all the terms used in them. They re-present a summary of the following chapter. In a *Sastra* this is one of the traditional methods in the art of connecting two consecutive chapters together. In the form of *mantras,* these two stanzas indicate the contents and the theme of the following chapter.

ॐ तत्सदिति श्रीमद्भगवद्गीतासूपनिषत्सु ब्रह्मविद्यायां
योगशास्त्रे श्रीकृष्णार्जुनसंवादे ज्ञानविज्ञानयोगो
नाम सप्तमोऽध्यायः ॥ ७ ॥

om tat-sat ity srimad bhagavadgitasupanisatsu
brahmavidyayam yogasastre
sri krisnarjunasamvade
Jnana vijnanayogo nama saptamodhyayah.

Thus, in the Upanishads of the glorious Bhagwad Geeta, in the Science of the Eternal, in the scripture of Yoga, in the dialogue between Sri Krishna and Arjuna, the seventh discourse ends entitled:

THE YOGA OF KNOWLEDGE AND WISDOM

The Vedantic ideologies, preached in the Upanishads had become, by the time of Vyasa, mere speculative narrations of poetic perfection, divorced from the actualities of life. The Hindus, thus estranged from the essential glory and strength of their culture, were to be resurrected by showing them the practical beauty and fire that lie concealed in the philosophical speculations. In this chapter, Krishna has emphasized and indicated beyond all doubts, how Vedantic perfection could be achieved and lived to the glory of the sucessful seeker and to the blessing of the generation in which he lived. It is most appropriate, therefore, that the chapter is named as *"The Yoga of Knowledge and Wisdom."*

Mere knowledge is of no practical use. Wisdom is the glow that Knowledge imparts to the individual. The fulfilment of knowledge in an individual is possible only when he becomes a Man of Wisdom. Knowledge can be imparted, but Wisdom cannot be given. The philosophical portion of all religions provides the knowledge, the instructional section of all religions provides techniques by which the knowledge can be assimilated and digested into the very texture of the devotees' inner lives, and thereby every religion seeks to create Men of Wisdom, who have fulfilled their lives, rectified their religion, and blessed their generation.